Pocket Hero

by

Pippa Goodhart

Illustrated by Zoografic

For Diane Wright
and the children of Oakham

KIRKLEES CULTURAL AND LEISURE SERVICES	
550 568 776	
Askews	08-Oct-2007
	£5.99
	CUL43781

First published in 2007 in Great Britain by
Barrington Stoke Ltd
18 Walker Street, Edinburgh, EH3 7LP

www.barringtonstoke.co.uk

ISBN: 978-1-84299-467-2

Printed in Great Britain by Bell & Bain Ltd

Contents

Chapter 1
'Freak of Nature'

Jeffrey Hudson was born very small. He was born almost 400 years ago on 14th June 1619. Jeffrey didn't grow like other children. The years passed, but Jeffrey only grew to 18 inches high. That's 45 cm, just over two times as high as this book. Jeffrey was born into a poor family who lived in a one-room home in a small town called

Oakham. But Jeffrey's life at home with his family didn't last long.

Jeffrey's father was a butcher called John Hudson. He had a new and important customer – the Duke of Buckingham. The Duke was a great friend of the King. He had moved into a very grand house just outside Oakham. That house was called Burley On The Hill and it had its own park.

John Hudson sold meat to the cook at the house. He also organised bull-baiting for the Duke when he wanted to entertain his visitors. Bull-baiting was a horrible sport where a bull was tied up and dogs were let loose to attack the bull. People bet on which would die first – the bull or one of the dogs. John Hudson sold the bulls to the Duke.

People did other strange things for fun. They seemed to enjoy seeing anything that they could call a 'freak of nature'. We know of fairs where there were tents with 'freaks' on show. There was one with a calf with five legs and another with a woman with a beard. A big London fair showed a dwarf kept in a parrot cage. It's likely that little Jeffrey was shown at local fairs or at inns. He would have stood on a table to be laughed at, and perhaps danced a little and people gave him a few pennies.

How else was a boy who was only 45 cm high going to make a living? Most poor children would have been working in the fields or helping their parents with work. Jeffrey was too small for that.

His family must have thought that Jeffrey would spend his life going round the country as one of those 'freaks'. But Jeffrey was lucky. Grand people liked those things too, and Jeffrey was about to be seen by the grandest people of all.

The Duke's wife got to hear about Jeffrey. Maybe she saw him one day with his father, bringing the meat to the Duke's kitchen? Perhaps she heard gossip about him or saw him at a fair. It was a fashion for rich people to have dwarfs working for them at that time. The Duke's wife wanted Jeffrey to come and live at Burley On The Hill.

So, aged just six or seven, Jeffrey left home to go and live with the Duke. Jeffrey went from wearing poor rough clothes to wearing clothes made of bright silk and velvet and lace. He went from eating cheese, bread and porridge to eating the finest foods and drinking wine. He had servants to look after him. Was he pleased to have become so much richer than his family were? Or was he upset to have been sent away from them? We don't know. But Jeffrey was soon going to be sent even further away and to live an even richer life.

King Charles had just got married to a 15-year-old French princess. The new Queen was called Henrietta. Queen Henrietta was about to become a very important person in Jeffrey's life.

Chapter 2
Baked in a Pie

Sing a song of sixpence
A pocket full of rye.
Four and twenty blackbirds
Baked in a pie.
When the pie was opened
The birds began to sing.
Wasn't that a dainty dish
To set before the King?

****

Jeffrey had sung that song along with other children, but he hadn't really thought about the words until the Duke's wife came to him one day with some news.

"Jeffrey, we're going to have a visitor."

"Who is that, my lady?" asked Jeffrey.

The Duke's wife sniffed a small bunch of flowers in her hand. "The Duke is to give a fine dinner to welcome the new Queen to England. Queen Henrietta is hardly more than a child, you know. She hardly speaks a word of English. How will we entertain the girl? The Duke has in mind a funny pie. You'll have heard the song about blackbirds being put into a pie to fly out and surprise people at table. Parrots and frogs have been put into pies as a joke. What a horrid mess they must have made! But your father thinks we can put something in a pie for Her Majesty that no-one has done before."

"And what's that, my lady?" asked Jeffrey.

"He thinks that a *person* should be put in the pie."

"A person in a pie? That can't be done!" Jeffrey said.

"It's true that nobody could ever fit *me* into a pie. Not in my skirts! But if the person were tiny enough, then it could be done. Which tiny person do you think your father says should be put in the pie?"

Jeffrey's eyes were big. "Not me, my lady?"

"Yes, you, Jeffrey. Isn't that exciting?"

"But I don't want to be cooked in a pie! I don't want to be eaten!"

The Duke's wife laughed, waved her bunch of flowers at Jeffrey and walked from the room.

****

So Jeffrey was taken by coach to the Duke's house in London. It must have taken two or three days to travel there. Jeffrey would have had to stand on the seat inside the coach if he wanted to look out of the windows. Think how Jeffrey might have felt being in London for the first time. London was a big city with thousands of houses, and hundreds of churches and other big buildings. The River Thames was full of boats. The sight of London must have been as amazing to Jeffrey as the sight of tiny

Jeffrey would have been to the people of London.

****

They took Jeffrey down to the kitchen. "We must see how you'll fit in the pie dish," they said.

"No!" Jeffrey struggled and bit and had to be carried all the way. Cook put her hands to her cheeks when she saw the tiny boy who hardly came up to her knees.

"Lord, who would have thought a person could be so tiny!"

Jeffrey was still fighting the big hands that held him.

"I won't be cut up and cooked!" yelled Jeffrey. "I won't!"

"Hush yourself," said the Cook. She bent down and prodded Jeffrey with a plump finger. She was testing to see if this doll-sized boy was real. "No-one is going to cook you, lad! The fun is all in you being alive and jumping out of the pie to give the Queen the surprise of her life! And you'll be looking like a smart soldier when you pop out of that pie. You might do a little dance or march about a bit to make the grand folk laugh."

Jeffrey stopped struggling. "I want to march," he said.

"Then we'd better dress you as a soldier fit for a queen," said Cook.

Chapter 3
Toy Soldier

They set little Jeffrey on the table. They fitted him with fine clothes and armour. And they made a flag for him to carry.

"Can I have a sword?" asked Jeffrey.

"So that you can cut yourself out of the pie from the inside if the Queen can't cut it from the outside?" the Cook said.

On the evening of the feast Jeffrey was dressed in his new outfit. He stepped with care into the pie, and lay in a curl at the bottom of it.

"Careful with that sword! Keep the flag in your hand, ready."

"Here comes the pie crust," warned Cook. "No poking or nibbling at the pastry, now! Lie still!"

The lid of pastry was put over the pie. It hid the light and shut off the air. It was dark inside the pie. It was soon stuffy in there, and the sounds from outside the pie were muffled. Jeffrey was breathing fast.

"Ready, Jeffrey?" asked Cook. "Keep still and wait for the sound of trumpets. When you hear those trumpets, you jump out. Everyone's eyes will be on the pie and on you."

The dish tipped like a boat at sea as the two footmen lifted the pie up high and carried it from the kitchen. Inside the pie, Jeffrey tried not to be afraid in the swaying darkness. He thought of how the golden crust of the pie must look glinting in the candle-light. He thought of the pie being put down on the table among the silver, the shining glasses and the golden plates. There would be fine foods and wine and flowers on the table. And all around the pie there would be eyes, watching. Two of those eyes would belong to the Queen of England, sitting with the King beside her.

The mumble of talk and the sway of music suddenly shushed. Jeffrey felt the jolt of the dish as it was put down onto the table. He heard the Duke's big voice saying to the Queen, "Your Majesty, I offer you a humble pie, but not a common one. Please, take up that knife and cut the pie open."

Jeffrey held his sword and flag tight. He looked up in the darkness, watching for the silver knife blade coming through the pastry. Then he heard the sound of trumpets, and in a moment Jeffrey was up on his knees, pushing up the pie crust to breathe in the air and dazzle his eyes with light. He lifted the pie crust, like the blankets from a bed. There were gasps of surprise all around him. Then Jeffrey climbed out of the pie and the sound exploded into cheering and hands thumping the table, making it shake. And all that noise was for Jeffrey.

Jeffrey jumped from the pie, and he held his flag high. He waved his sword at the people looking down all around him. Jeffrey kicked an apricot, and he stuck his sword into a plum, and everyone cheered even louder. Jeffrey began to march up and down the long table. The people laughed now, all of them apart from the girl who

was holding the knife. Her face was at the same level as Jeffrey's, and she smiled kindly.

"'Ello," she said. "What name you are called, leetle man?"

Jeffrey looked into the eyes of a girl who knew very well how it felt to be looked at and laughed at.

Jeffrey bowed low. "I am Jeffrey, your Majesty."

And the girl-queen turned to the Duke and said, "This leetle man, I want him for my own."

The Duke smiled smugly, and said, "Then he's yours, your majesty."

****

And that is how Jeffrey, aged only seven, became the Queen's pet. That dinner had cost over £5000. Jeffrey's family back in Oakham probably lived on less than £10 a year.

Chapter 4
The Queen's Dwarf

Jeffrey went to live with Queen Henrietta in a house where he wasn't the only pet. There were animal pets – birds and dogs and a monkey. And there were people pets. There were a man and a woman dwarf who were married to each other. But little Jeffrey was the one who became known as 'The Queen's Dwarf'. The Queen had a giant too. He was a man called William Evans and he was seven foot six inches tall. That's 2 m 30 cm – more than five times as tall as Jeffrey!

Queen Henrietta loved grand parties, called 'masques'. Masques were very long plays with amazing costumes, music, acrobats and actors. The Queen often took part in the masques herself. She made Jeffrey perform in them too. Jeffrey's first masque took place only two weeks after he stepped out of the pie. Jeffrey had to hide in the giant's pocket. The giant came onto the stage and sat down. He pulled a loaf of bread from one pocket. Then he put a hand into his other pocket. We are told by someone who saw it that William 'drew little Jeffrey the Dwarf from his pocket, first to the wonder, then to the laughter of the beholders'. Jeffrey's main job at court was to be funny, to be laughed at.

Jeffrey had servants. He was taught to read and write. He learned to speak French like his mistress, the Queen. He learned how to ride a horse and how to shoot a pistol. He learned how to dance. There are pictures painted of Jeffrey and poems written about him. In one of those poems, Jeffrey is called 'Lord Minimus' because he was a mini grand gentleman. He was famous and well cared for.

But Jeffrey's life was soon to be put in danger. When he was ten years old, Jeffrey set out on what turned into a real adventure.

In 1629 Queen Henrietta had a baby boy. The baby was called Charles, after his father. But the baby died when he was just one hour old. When Queen Henrietta became pregnant again, she wanted a mid-wife from the French court to be with her for the next birth. She sent an odd group of people to France to collect the mid-wife and some French monks. She sent the people who organised her parties. She sent her 'Master of Ceremonies' and her Dancing Master, and Jeffrey. Why Jeffrey? Henrietta wanted to show the French King, what she enjoyed at the English court. The French King was her brother. The Queen's French family must have heard of the famous tiny boy. Perhaps they had asked to see him.

Jeffrey had never been on a ship before. It was exciting to be out on the sea, but it made Jeffrey feel sick. He wasn't tall enough to see over the side as the sailors told him to. But he was longing to see the country that Queen Henrietta had told him so much about.

When Jeffrey arrived at the French court, there was lots of pointing and laughing at him at first. But most of the laughter was kind. Queen Henrietta's mother, Marie de Medici, liked Jeffrey very much.

"So very tiny in body, but so very big and clever in himself!" she said.

The ladies of the French court were so taken with Jeffrey that they gave him £2,000 worth of jewels. That was a fortune for a child who was the son of a humble butcher.

Chapter 5
Pirates!

When it was time to go back home to England, Jeffrey's jewels were packed up. People and their bags were taken to a town called Calais, ready to board a ship.

"What kind of boat is that?" asked Jeffrey, pointing at the slim ship with three masts and lots of sails hanging from each one.

"It's called a barque, Sir," said the French captain. "A fast ship. You will be back in England in a matter of hours."

But the captain was wrong.

Out on the open sea, they saw another ship. Jeffrey watched, wanting to see what kind of a ship it was that was coming closer and closer. Then suddenly,

"Pirates!" yelled a sailor from the rigging.

"Where have they come from?" asked Jeffrey.

"They're pirates from Dunkirk, Master Jeffrey. Quick! Get below where you can't be seen!"

Master Garnier, the Queen's Master of Ceremonies, was on deck. His wife was

Jeffrey's nurse. "Down below, everyone, and keep silent!" he ordered.

Jeffrey and the others were helped through the hatch down the steep steps to the darkness below decks. Jeffrey hid in a room with the ladies and the monks and the boxes of jewels and other gifts being sent to the English court. The monks prayed, and Jeffrey tried to pray too. But there was a sudden bump and the ship lurched.

"They've hit us!" said someone, and one of the ladies screamed.

"What will they do?" asked Jeffrey. Part of him wanted to run back up the steps and see what pirates looked like. Part of him just wanted to hide.

There was the sound of feet banging down the steps. One of the ladies held

Jeffrey tight to her. Men burst into the cabin, yelling. The pirates grabbed the four ladies.

"Leave them alone!" shouted Jeffrey, and he ran at the pirates and he punched one of them behind the knees, making him fall with a thump. For a moment everyone was silent.

"Who did that?" shouted a big man with a beard. He was looking around for the person who had done it. Jeffrey saw that there was a pistol in his hand. The fallen man pointed at Jeffrey. The man with the gun gasped. Then he began to do what everyone always did. He laughed. He put away his gun. He grabbed Jeffrey and carried him up on deck and into their pirate ship. Jeffrey saw the crates of jewels and money being taken too.

"Robbers!" said Jeffrey, and he tried to twist free. "That money is mine!"

"Shush!" said Master Garnier. "Don't anger them, Jeffrey, or who knows what they might do to us."

The pirates kept the treasure, but they set the people free. Soon Jeffrey and the others were put onto another ship which took them safely home to England.

The Queen was delighted to have her midwife and her monks and her dwarf safe with her. She gave Jeffrey £2,000 of her own money to make up for what he had lost. And she ordered a new painting to be done of Jeffrey.

****

Two months later Queen Henrietta gave birth to another baby boy called Charles. This child would grow up to become King Charles the Second.

Chapter 6
War

For a time life went on happily. The
King and Queen enjoyed beautiful and
expensive things. In 1633, the King invited
an artist called Van Dyck to come to
England to paint the royal family. One
picture shows Queen Henrietta with Jeffrey
beside her. Jeffrey is dressed in red velvet
with lace collar and cuffs. He is wearing
riding boots and spurs. The Queen's pet
monkey is on his shoulder. Jeffrey was 14

years old when the picture was painted. He doesn't look so very tiny in the picture, but that is because he is next to the Queen. Henrietta was small, under 5 feet tall, and she was wearing high heels. Jeffrey is painted looking up at the Queen, in the same way that a dog might look at its owner. But Jeffrey was beginning to want to be more than just a human pet.

When he was 18, Jeffrey saw real fighting for the first time. Holland and Spain were at war. Jeffrey went with some friends to Holland to see the war being fought there. It was a shock after the kind of life that he was used to.

Back home things were changing too. The people of England were getting very angry with the King. He wanted money to fight a war. But the people didn't want war, and they didn't want to pay more money. People wanted to have some say in how their money was spent. But the King wouldn't allow that. So he tried to get money and soldiers another way. He did a deal with the Dutch royal family. In return for money and soldiers, King Charles gave his eldest daughter as a bride for the Dutch Prince. Prince William was only twelve years old. Poor Princess Mary was only nine. At their wedding party, Jeffrey played the part of the clown at court for the last time. He was 21. He was still tiny, but he was a man now.

Civil war broke out in England. Jeffrey stayed close to the Queen, sometimes fighting to protect her. When Queen Henrietta escaped to Holland, Jeffrey went with her. There was a great storm at sea and some of the ships were sunk. In Holland, the Queen got together money and guns to take back to England. But on their way back they were hit by another storm and more ships were sunk. Still, the little

French lady who was the English Queen was tough.

Back in England she put together a big army with thousands of soldiers and 150 wagons of food and drink. Queen Henrietta made tiny Jeffrey Hudson her army's 'Captain of Horse'. Jeffrey was in charge of a large number of soldiers and horses. The army marched to Oxford, to join the King's own army and the boy princes, Prince Charles and Prince James. The country was at war, and 'Captain' Jeffrey Hudson, under two foot high, was now a soldier and a leader.

Battles followed. We don't know how much of a part Jeffrey took in the fighting. Prince Charles and Prince James, who were only children, fought in battles. They rode on horses and Jeffrey probably did too. Being so small wasn't such a problem if you were up on a horse and had a gun in your hand.

The war didn't go well for the King, and the Queen was ill. In April 1644, Queen Henrietta, Jeffrey and a few other servants left Oxford. On their journey south, they stopped, and the Queen gave birth to a baby girl. The baby was called Princess Henriette-Anne. The Queen and Jeffrey escaped to France leaving the new baby behind. The baby was smuggled to France to join the Queen soon afterwards. But the Queen would never see her husband, the King, again. Princess Henriette-Anne never met her father. Jeffrey wouldn't return to England for more than 25 years.

Chapter 7
The Duel

The Queen was allowed into France, but she wasn't very welcome. She and her servants had to keep moving from place to place. The Queen was ill and worried about her husband and children. It was no fun for Jeffrey either. Some young English men had left England to join the Queen. But they were bored and silly and drank too much wine.

****

"Hey, Dwarf!" shouted one of them. "I hear that you're a soldier these days. Is that right?"

"It is," said Jeffrey.

"What sort of horse would fit such a titch? Do you ride a rat? Do you carry a tooth-pick for a sword? An acorn for a helmet?"

The young men laughed. But Jeffrey didn't.

"Gentlemen," said Jeffrey. "If any of you don't think I can fight, let me prove it."

"Ooo, I *am* scared!" said one of them, pretending to shake with fear. "What do you intend to do to us?"

"The next man to insult me can face me in a duel," said Jeffrey. The men laughed even louder.

"Then, my Lord Flea," said a man called Crofts, "You had better fight me."

They arrived at the park at dawn on a misty morning, and the duel began.

"Name your weapons!"

"I have mine here, sir," said Crofts. He pulled out a water squirt from under his coat. "We shall fight with water!"

Crofts and his friends laughed at the joke. But Jeffrey didn't.

"We will fight with pistols!" he said.

Jeffrey and Charles sat on horses a hundred yards apart. A white cloth was held high, then dropped as the signal to charge. The horses galloped towards one another. And at last Crofts saw that Jeffrey had the advantage. Jeffrey had by far the bigger target to aim at. Jeffrey raised his pistol. He shot Crofts through the head. Crofts fell from his horse, dead. And then no-one was laughing.

Jeffrey won his duel. But duels were against the law in France, and Crofts had a brother who was an important man. When Queen Henrietta heard what had happened, she told Jeffrey that he must leave. So Jeffrey fled. He hoped to get back to England and fight for his King again. But that wasn't going to happen. Jeffrey never had much luck in boats at sea, and this time his luck was worse than ever.

****

Out at sea, the cry went out,

"Ship ahoy!"

That cry was soon followed by other shouts.

"Pirates!"

Jeffrey's heart thudded with the memory of being kidnapped by Dunkirk pirates 15 years before. But these pirates were not from Dunkirk.

"Barbary Pirates!" went the shout. "Get below!"

As Jeffrey made his way towards the hatch, he saw three boats called "galleys". They were low and slim and sleek in the water, coming fast. The galleys had sails, but they had oars as well, sticking out of the sides of the boats like insect legs. There was panic on deck. People were running and shouting. Then – crash! – the leading galley rammed the ship. Jeffrey fell onto the deck, and then – boom! – a cannon on the galley fired at them.

Jeffrey tumbled down the hatch. He hid in a corner and heard thuds, screams, gun-shots, and foot-steps above him. He felt the pirates leap onto the ship, and soon they were crashing down the steps and grabbing

Jeffrey and others as their captives. These pirates spoke in a strange language. They were dressed in clothes that Jeffrey had never seen before. And they carried great glinting curved swords.

Jeffrey had heard tales of these Barbary Pirates. What they stole was people.

Chapter 8
Slavery

Jeffrey was tossed onto one of the galleys, then his hands were tied.

"We'll be sold as slaves!" said someone.

"We'll be rowing galleys like this one," said a sailor. Jeffrey looked at the men chained and sweating beside their oars. He looked at the man with the whip who was in charge of them, and he was terrified.

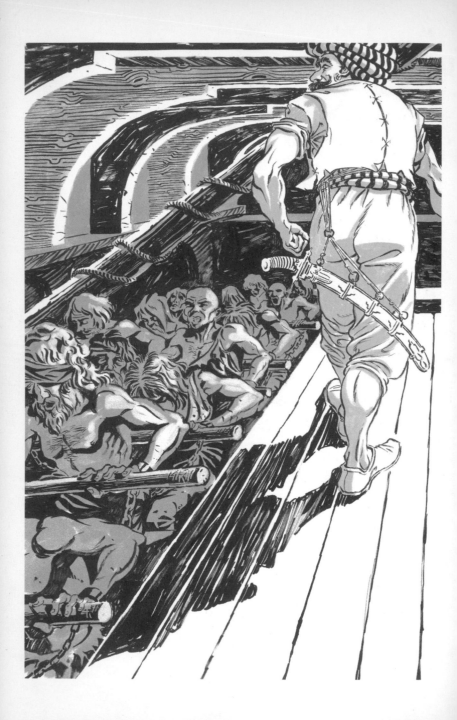

"Don't worry, sir. You'll be of no use for that job," said a kind sailor. "You'll be sold as a slave in Africa. I expect they'd like an odd one like you to serve their friends."

****

Jeffrey was taken to Africa. It was a hot, strange country that he knew nothing about. He was with people who spoke a language he didn't understand. The people round him ate different foods and had different gods and wore different clothes. Jeffrey was terrified.

No one knows what happened to Jeffrey in Africa. He was probably taken to Algiers in North Africa. There were about 25,000 slaves in Algiers at that time. Jeffrey would have been put in chains and sold at a slave market. The only hope for freedom was if somebody back in England got to know where Jeffrey was and sent money to buy him back. But who could do that? Nobody knew where Jeffrey was. And England was at war against itself. So 25-year-old Jeffrey began 25 years of life as a slave.

We don't know what sort of owner or owners Jeffrey had during his time as a slave. He may well have been bought as a 'freak' because of his small size. But something strange happened to Jeffrey while he was in Africa. He began to grow. So, by the time he came back to England, he was twice as old and twice as tall as he had been when he left. Aged 50, he was 1 m 12 cm tall – still oddly tiny, but no longer doll-sized.

England had changed too. While Jeffrey was in Africa, England killed its King. King Charles the First had his head chopped off in 1649. For 11 years the country was ruled without a king. But in 1660 Prince Charles became the new King, Charles the Second.

His mother, Queen Henrietta, came back to England for a while. She had a Chinese boy now as her new 'pet'. She returned to France and died before Jeffrey came back to England.

When 50 year old Jeffrey came home to England, he went to live with one of his brothers back in Oakham. Ten years later, when his brother died, Jeffrey travelled back to London. But London was very different from the city he had known. The Great Plague and the Great Fire of London had changed things. And the royal court did not want an old dwarf who was not as tiny as he had been before.

Worst of all, people were afraid that Catholics were trying to kill the King. Because Jeffrey had been brought up by Henrietta, who was a Catholic, people didn't trust him. He was put in prison.

Poor Jeffrey was stuck in prison for two years. When he came out of prison, King Charles gave him some money to live off. But Jeffrey died soon afterwards. He was 62.

Jeffrey Hudson lived a life of extremes. He lived as a poor man and a rich man. He was a clown and a soldier, a man of power and then a slave and a prisoner. He was an amazing man.

Epilogue

There are pictures and writing from the time which show that the story of Jeffrey Hudson is true. But I still didn't quite believe that he could have been put into a pie until I looked at some old recipes.

There is a strange recipe from about 30 years before Jeffrey's pie was made. The recipe is 'To make Pies that the Birds may be alive in them, and flie out when it is cut up'.

The recipe tells you to make what it calls a 'coffin' of pastry. Pastry in those days was very hard and strong. Often it wasn't meant to be eaten. Pastry just made a kind of pot to cook meat and fruit in. The pastry 'coffin' was shaped around a big dish, and then cooked until it was hard. The lid could be cooked by itself too.

So there was no need to cook birds or small boys! They were simply put alive into the big round pastry pot, and the lid put on top. For a grand feast the lid of the pie would be made pretty with real gold leaf and pastry shapes.

We know that very big pies were made when there were lots of people to feed. There is another pie recipe in which the pie is filled with a whole turkey stuffed with a goose stuffed with three smaller birds, each smaller than the other. Any gaps in that pie were to be filled with rabbit meat and four pounds of butter. A pastry case big enough to hold that lot would have been big enough to hold an 18-inch high boy!

Barrington Stoke would like to thank all its readers for commenting on the manuscript before publication and in particular:

Hannah Berrisford
Michelle Brady
Andrew Bragg
Holly Bramman
Leon Brown
Marjory Brown
Nathan Burton
Ryan Campbell
Jack Carrny
Shirley D. Davids
Sophie Dennet
George Dennis
Ebony Flexon-Bennet
Kieron Fortune
Kate Foster
Francesca Gee
Ronnan Griffiths
Katie Hayes
Wilf Henson
Graeme Hume
Mark Hunter
Graeme Johnstone
Sam Kelly
Elliot Lorriman

Chris Madagba
Alwyn Martin
Billy Metcalfe
Cameron Murphy
Kady Parr
Harriet Phillips
Billy Quinn
Ellie Ratcliffe
Phoebe Robb
Emily Sargant
Jessie Sargent
Amber Sedgwick
Caitlin Sheppard
Timothy Small
Christopher Smith
Jess Snowden
George Thorpe
Ryan Tonkin
Josephine White
William White
Sandie Whyte
Nathan Williamson
Thomas Woodhouse
William Yildiz

Become a Consultant!

Would you like to give us feedback on our titles before they are published? Contact us at the e-mail address below – we'd love to hear from you!

info@barringtonstoke.co.uk
www.barringtonstoke.co.uk

AUTHOR CHECK LIST

Pippa Goodhart

If *you* could go anywhere, at any point in history, where would it be?
I'd go back and meet my father when he was a little boy.

Who can you think of in the past who was as great a hero as Jeffrey Hudson?
Mary Read was a woman from England who went to sea and fought as a man. Later she got married, but after her husband died, she went back to sea again!

Who do you think is the scariest villain in history?
Stalin and Hitler are two of the most scary.

If you could choose, would you rather fight a man in a duel or get caught by pirates?
I'd rather be caught by pirates. In a duel you have to kill someone or get killed yourself. No thank you. With pirates, you might be able to run away.

If you could invite anyone famous from history to a party, who would it be?
I'd invite Mozart to play lovely music, Oscar Wilde to tell funny stories, and Jeffrey Hudson so that I could share a big pie with him!

ILLUSTRATOR CHECK LIST

Zoografic

If you could choose, would you rather fight a man in a duel or get caught by pirates?

Chris: Fight in a duel, steal the treasure and get the princess.

David: Me, fight in a duel? Only if I had no choice ... maybe for something that was worth it ...

If *you* could go anywhere, at any point in history, where would it be?

Chris: I would like to travel in an adventure book that I have read before and then I would try to change the ending.

David: It would be great to travel to all the distant corners of the Solar System, surfing the Saturn rings ...

Who can you think of in the past who was as great a hero as Jeffrey Hudson?

Chris: The greatest swashbuckler is Zorro, without a doubt.

Try another book in the
REALITY CHECK
series

The Land Of Whizzing Arrows
by Simon Chapman

Escape From Colditz
by Deborah Chancellor

The Last Duel
by Martyn Beardsley

Dick Turpin: Legends and Lies
by Terry Deary

All available from our website:
www.barringtonstoke.co.uk